THE YOUNG PERSON'S GUIDE TO

SHAKESPEARE

THE YOUNG PERSON'S GUIDE TO

SHAKESPEARE

IN ASSOCIATION WITH

THE ROYAL SHAKESPEARE COMPANY

ANITA GANERI

Chrysalis Children's Books

PUBLISHED IN BRITAIN IN 2004 BY
CHRYSALIS CHILDREN'S BOOKS
AN IMPRINT OF CHRYSALIS BOOKS GROUP PLC
THE CHRYSALIS BUILDING
BRAMLEY ROAD, LONDON W10 6SP

FIRST PUBLISHED IN BRITAIN IN 1999

Editorial Manager: JOYCE BENTLEY
Consultant: KATHY ELGIN, ROYAL SHAKESPEARE COMPANY
Designer: NIGEL PARTRIDGE
Editor: JO FLETCHER-WATSON

SET IN ITC GARAMOND
PRINTED IN CHINA

2 4 6 8 10 9 7 5 3 1

*(frontispiece) The final scene from a RSC production
of* Much Ado About Nothing

Contents

Introduction

A great welcome to the fascinating world of William Shakespeare. In Shakespeare's time, going to the theatre was the most popular form of entertainment, in the same way as going to the cinema or watching a sports event is today. Almost 400 years later, Shakespeare's plays are still incredibly popular throughout the world, making him the most performed, printed, and translated playwright ever. Shakespeare's work has inspired many films, plays, and books, bringing his beautiful language and finely drawn plots and characters to a modern audience. His work is read by millions of students in schools and universities worldwide.

This book looks at Shakespeare's life in Stratford and London and at his flourishing career, first as an actor, then as a playwright. Read about Shakespeare's major works and meet his most famous characters. Find out how Shakespeare is performed in the theatre, from the selection of a play to the rising curtain on opening night. This book includes some of Shakespeare's best-known speeches, which are printed on pages 50–52. *The Young Person's Guide to Shakespeare* is the perfect introduction to the life and work of the world's most famous playwright.

(left) A scene from The Tempest *by the Cuban Theatre Company at the Teatro Buendía*

Who was Shakespeare?

William Shakespeare wrote some of the best-known plays and poems in the English language. His beautiful language and universal themes of love, ambition, and jealousy make his work as popular and relevant today as when it was written nearly 400 years ago.

When did Shakespeare live?

Shakespeare lived from 1564 to 1616 in England, during the reigns of Elizabeth I (1558–1603) and James I (1603–1625). It was a golden age for theatre going. Many actors became rich and famous. The first permanent theatres in London were built, and audiences flocked to the plays. There was plenty of work for budding playwrights, especially those as gifted as Shakespeare. This was also the golden age of exploration, when sailors and traders from Europe ventured to undiscovered parts of the world. The name of Shakespeare's theatre, the Globe, reflected that spirit of adventure.

A well-known portrait of Shakespeare, painted by John Taylor

What do we know about Shakespeare?

There are very few written records about Shakespeare or his family. None of the original manuscripts of his plays, poems, or sonnets has survived. The only remaining examples of Shakespeare's own handwriting are six versions of his signature from his will and other legal documents.

(far left) A more romantic portrayal of Shakespeare, painted by Soest

(left) Queen Elizabeth I

Performing Shakespeare

All over the world, Shakespeare's plays are performed more often than those of any other playwright in history. They have influenced hundreds of films, musicals, ballets, and operas. More than 300 film versions of the major plays have been produced. Playing a Shakespearean role is often the greatest challenge of an actor's career.

Shakespeare's Early Life

Shakespeare, the third of eight children, was born in Stratford-upon-Avon, a market town in Warwickshire, England. His father, John, was a glove maker and a dealer in wool and property. His mother, Mary Arden, was the daughter of a wealthy local landowner.

Shakespeare's school days

From the age of eleven onwards, Shakespeare probably attended King Edward VI Grammar School in Stratford. There he developed his love of literature, both ancient and modern, which later served him well in his work as a playwright. Around the age of fifteen, he left school and started working for his father. He did not go to university.

The Henley Street house where Shakespeare was born

(above) The school room of King Edward VI Grammar School, Stratford, as it would have been in Shakespeare's day

SHAKESPEARE'S STRATFORD

Many of the places associated with the life of Shakespeare in Stratford have been preserved and can be visited today.

◆ **Shakespeare's birthplace**
Shakespeare was born in a house in Henley Street. Part of the house is furnished as it would have been in Shakespeare's time.

◆ **New Place and Nash's House**
Shakespeare's family home from 1597 until his death. Only the site and foundations remain. Next door is Nash's House, which belonged to Thomas Nash, who was the first husband of

DID YOU KNOW?

Traditionally, Shakespeare's birthday is celebrated as April 23, 1564, although we do not know the exact date on which he was born. Coincidentally, he died on April 23, 1616.

Shakespeare's only granddaughter, called Elizabeth.

◆ **Hall's Croft**

The home of Shakespeare's daughter, Susanna, and her husband, Dr. John Hall, before they moved to New Place after Shakespeare's death

◆ **Anne Hathaway's cottage**

Anne's home before her marriage to Shakespeare, in the village of Shottery near Stratford

◆ **Mary Arden's house**

The farmhouse where Shakespeare's mother grew up, in the village of Wilmcote near Stratford

Anne Hathaway's cottage

Getting married

On November 27, 1582, aged eighteen, Shakespeare married Anne Hathaway, the daughter of a farmer from nearby Shottery. She was twenty-six and pregnant at the time of their marriage. Their first daughter, Susanna, was christened on May 26, 1583. Two years later Anne gave birth to twins, Hamnet and Judith. Hamnet died in 1596, aged eleven.

The lost years

By 1592 Shakespeare had left Stratford for London and was making his name as an actor and playwright. We do not know what happened in the so-called "lost years" before that, between 1585 and 1592. According to various stories, Shakespeare worked as a schoolmaster, soldier, or lawyer, or he joined a touring company of actors visiting Stratford.

DID YOU KNOW?

Before permanent theatres began to be built in London in the 1570s, groups of actors travelled from town to town performing the latest plays. When Shakespeare's father was mayor of Stratford, he encouraged these companies to perform in the town. Shakespeare would have seen these plays, which may have inspired his love of theatre.

Shakespeare in London

In Shakespeare's day, London was a thriving city of nearly 200,000 people. It was crowded and dirty, with great contrast between the lives of rich and poor. On arriving in London, Shakespeare found lodgings in Bishopsgate but then moved to Bankside to be closer to the theatres.

The first theatres

The first permanent indoor theatre building was constructed in Shoreditch in east London in 1576. It was called The Theatre. Before this, plays were often performed in the yards of taverns and inns. In 1587 the Rose Theatre was built in Bankside, followed by the Swan (1594–1595) and the Globe (1599). The Swan, which held 3,000 people, was described as the biggest and finest theatre in London.

ENTERTAINMENTS

In addition to the theatre, the Elizabethans loved bear- and bull-baiting, cockfighting, and watching public executions. This is how one eyewitness described a visit to the Bear Garden in Bankside:

"There is a round building, three stories high, in which are kept about a hundred large English dogs, with separate wooden kennels for each of them. These dogs were made to fight singly with three bears, the second bear being larger than the first and the third larger than the second. After this, a bull was brought in and chased by the dogs, and at last a bull who defended himself most bravely."

Bear-baiting was a brutal but popular pastime in Elizabethan times.

A painting of London in the 1600s viewed from the south bank of the River Thames

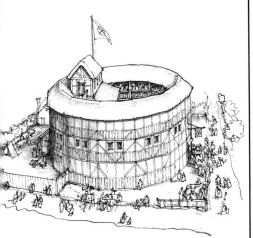

(above) What the Rose Theatre would have looked like in Shakespeare's day. The raised flag indicates that a play is about to begin

(right) An artist's impression of London's Southbank in Elizabethan times, showing the position of the theatres

DID YOU KNOW?

To cross the river to the theatres, people could hail a small ferry boat, called a wherry. They knew which way the wherry was heading by the ferryman's cry of "Westward ho!" or "Eastward ho!" A plan to move the theatres north of the river was blocked by the ferrymen because such a move would have been bad for their business.

Bankside

The theatres were deliberately built outside the walls of the city of London to remain outside the strict control of the city authorities, who claimed that plays had a bad effect on people's morals. Bankside, close to London Bridge on the south bank of the River Thames, was notorious for its brothels, gambling dens, taverns, and low life.

Company of actors

Each theatre had its own company of actors and was sponsored by a wealthy patron. Shakespeare joined the Lord Chamberlain's Men. In 1603 the company became the King's Men, with King James himself as their patron. Shakespeare worked first as an actor and director and later as chief playwright. Along with the other leading actors, he also owned shares in the company and in the Globe Theatre.

The Great Wooden O

In 1599 Shakespeare and the Lord Chamberlain's Men took up residence in a new theatre on Bankside. It was called the Globe. *As You Like It* is thought to have been their first production.

The original Globe, as it appeared in Claus Jan Visscher's View of London, *in 1616*

Building the Globe

The Globe was built from the timbers of The Theatre in Shoreditch, the previous home of the Lord Chamberlain's Men. The landlord had refused to renew the lease so, under cover of night, the actors dismantled The Theatre beam by beam, secretly ferried it across the river, and had it rebuilt in Bankside. Because it was partly open to the sky, the Globe could be used only in summer. From October to April, when the Globe was closed, the Globe's actors performed in an indoor playhouse at Blackfriars.

What the Globe looked like

In the prologue to *Henry V*, Shakespeare himself describes the Globe as "this wooden O." In fact, the theatre was not completely round but had five sides. It was half-timbered, with a thatched roof above the more expensive gallery seats. Around the stage was the open yard where audience members, called groundlings, could stand and watch the play. The stage, sheltered by an ornate ceiling, extended into the middle of the yard, so the groundlings were always closest to the action. The staging area probably had trapdoors in the flooring and primitive rigging overhead. When full, the theatre held around 2,500 people.

An artist's impression of Queen Elizabeth I watching The Merry Wives of Windsor *inside the Globe Theatre*

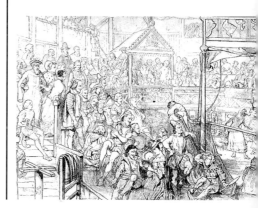

Disaster strikes

O n June 29, 1613, during a performance of *Henry VIII*, disaster struck. A cannon on the stage backfired and set the thatched roof on fire. In less than an hour, the theatre burned to the ground. Incredibly, no one was hurt, although one man's breeches caught on fire! The Globe was rebuilt in 1614 and was soon back in business. But it was closed by the Puritans in 1642 and demolished two years later.

The new Globe in London

The new Globe

I n 1996, just a stone's throw away from the site of the original theatre, a brand-new Globe opened its doors to the public. The brainchild of the American actor and director Sam Wanamaker, it took almost ten years to build. Audiences can now see Shakespeare's plays performed in the theatre for which they were written.

A Visit to the Theatre

Elizabethans flocked to the theatre to see the latest plays and to cheer or boo the actors. The most popular form of entertainment at the time, theatre going was for everyone, ordinary people as well as the rich.

Performance times

Because the theatres had no artificial lighting, performances were held in the afternoon, beginning at 2:00 P.M. A silk flag was flown above the theatre to show that a performance would be staged that day. Just before the play began, a trumpet was blown to hurry theatre goers along. There were performances every day of the year except on Sundays and during Lent.

Elizabethans enjoying a visit to the Globe in Shakespeare's time, painted by George Pycroft

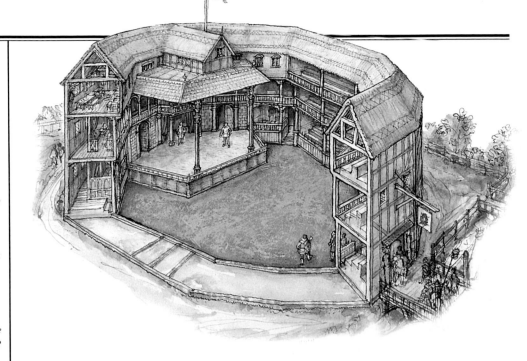

An artist's impression of the Rose
Theatre after alterations in 1592

Seats and prices

The cheapest tickets cost a penny. This brought standing room in the yard around the stage where the groundlings stood. For twopence you could sit in the lower gallery. Sixpence bought a seat in the upper gallery or on the stage itself. A "gentleman's room," or box, cost one shilling, which was a lot of money at the time.

Audience participation

Elizabethan audiences were not as well behaved as modern theatre goers. They talked, ate, and drank throughout the play, sang along to the songs, and sometimes even jumped on to the stage and joined in the sword fights. If they did not like what they saw, they booed and threw rotten fruit at the actors!

DID YOU KNOW?

A group of actors called gatherers stood at theatre doors to collect the ticket money, which was then locked away in a box. This is where we get the term *box office* – what we call a theatre ticket office today.

An Actor's Life

Being an actor in Shakespeare's day was very hard work. Each company put on several plays a week, and an actor rarely performed the same role for two days in a row.

Becoming an actor

Many actors started in children's companies. Others went straight into adult companies, between the ages of ten and thirteen. Women were not allowed to act, so female parts were played by young boys. Most actors had little training, although some were apprenticed to senior actors. There was a pecking order. At the bottom were the boy apprentices. Then came the "hired men," who acted as extras and backstage staff. At the top were the "sharers," who had money invested in the company.

In this authentic Elizabethan production of Henry V at the new Globe, London. Princess Katharine and the French Queen are both played by men

*Life's but a walking shadow, a poor player
The struts and frets his hour upon the stage,
And then is heard no more.*
(Macbeth, Macbeth, Act V, sc. v, 23–25)

Richard Burbage

Leading actors

The most famous actors in Shakespeare's company included:

RICHARD BURBAGE (1567–1619)

Sharer, manager, and leading actor of tragic roles.

Shakespeare wrote many of his tragic heroes, including Hamlet, Macbeth, Othello, and Richard III, especially for Burbage.

NATHAN FIELD (1587–1620)

An actor and playwright who started his career in a children's company. Field took Shakespeare's place in the King's Men in 1615. He wrote two plays of his own and collaborated on others.

Nathan Field

WILLIAM KEMPE (?–1603)

The main comedian in the company. Kempe played clowns and fools, including Dogberry in *Much Ado About Nothing*. He left the Lord Chamberlain's Men in 1599, perhaps because Shakespeare did not like his habit of making up his own lines instead of reciting those that had been written.

THEATRE PROPS

Little scenery was used onstage and the costumes and props set the scene. No records of the Globe's props remain, but an inventory exists from the Rose:

◆ Item, 1 rock, 1 cage, 1 tomb, 1 Hell Mouth
◆ Item, 2 steeples, and 1 chime of bells, and 1 beacon
◆ Item, 1 Globe, and 1 golden sceptre; 3 clubs
◆ Item, 2 marchpanes and the city of Rome
◆ Item, 1 Golden fleece, 2 rackets, 1 bay tree
◆ Item, 1 wooden canopy; old Mahomet's head
◆ Item, 8 vizards (masks)
◆ Item, Cupid's bow, and quiver; the cloth of the sun and moon
◆ Item, 2 mossy banks and one snake

An actor's day

Actors worked incredibly hard. With so many plays to perform, there was little time to learn lines or rehearse. In addition to having excellent memories, actors were also expected to sing, dance, play musical instruments, and fence. With no time to develop individual characters, actors were often typecast, playing the same type of character in play after play.

Plays and Playwriting

Shakespeare quickly earned fame and fortune for his hugely popular plays, and the public demand for new plays kept him busy. Shakespeare wrote about two plays each season, often continuing to work on a play while it was being rehearsed for performance.

Appearing at court

S hakespeare's company was always welcome at court and regularly performed for Elizabeth I and later for James I. A temporary stage was built inside one of the royal palaces. The monarch sat on a raised seat, or "state," to watch. Plays were strictly censored by the Revels Office to ensure they did not contain anything that would be offensive to the monarch.

(above) Edward Alleyn, one of the greatest actors of Shakespeare's day

(left) A play being acted in court for Queen Elizabeth I

DID YOU KNOW?

The playwright John Fletcher (1579–1625) probably collaborated with Shakespeare on *Henry VIII*, and Shakespeare may have helped with Fletcher's play *The Two Noble Kinsmen*. A third collaboration, *Gardenio*, was performed in 1613, but all written copies have been lost.

Ben Jonson

Rebellion and *Richard II*

Richard II was probably first performed in front of Queen Elizabeth's chief minister, Sir Robert Cecil, in December 1596. The scene in which the king is deposed by Bolingbroke was thought too sensitive and cut. In 1601 the Earl of Essex commissioned the Lord Chamberlain's Men to perform the uncensored play on the day before his planned rebellion against the queen. The rebellion failed, Essex was beheaded, and the Lord Chamberlain's Men were lucky to escape punishment themselves.

Fellow playwrights

Other popular playwrights in Shakespeare's time included:

BEN JONSON (1572–1637)
A leading dramatist, Jonson was also a great friend of Shakespeare. He, too, started his career as an actor, then turned to writing plays. He was named poet laureate in 1616.
GREATEST WORKS: *Volpone; The Silent Women; The Alchemist*

CHRISTOPHER MARLOWE (1564–1593)
The principal writer for the Rose Theatre, Marlowe wrote many heroic parts for the great actor Edward Alleyn. He was often in trouble with the authorities and was arrested several times. At the age of twenty-nine, he was stabbed to death in a tavern brawl.
GREATEST WORKS: *Tamburlaine; The Jew of Malta; Doctor Faustus*

THOMAS KYD (1558–1594)
The author of *The Spanish Tragedy*, the most popular of Elizabethan tragedies, Kyd set a trend for bloody tales of revenge. He was arrested and tortured for holding unorthodox religious and moral views but was released after implicating his friend Marlowe. He died shortly afterward.
GREATEST WORKS: *The First Part of Hieronimo; The Spanish Tragedy*

Shakespeare Retires

In 1611 or 1612, about a year before the disastrous fire at the Globe, Shakespeare returned to live in Stratford with his family. Although he is thought to have retired from writing, he remained friends with many actors and playwrights and continued to visit London.

Living in New Place

New Place

Shakespeare settled in New Place, a house he bought in 1597. He was now a wealthy man, and New Place was said to be the second finest house in Stratford. It was the only house made of brick and had two gardens, two orchards, and two barns. Shakespeare still spent most of his time working in London but finally settled at New Place in 1610. His elder daughter, Susanna, had married John Hall, a highly respected herbalist and doctor, in 1607. They lived in another fine house, Hall's Croft. His younger daughter, Judith, married Thomas Quiney in 1616.

Our revels now are ended. These our actors,
As I foretold you, were all spirits, and
Are melted into air, into thin air;
And like the baseless fabric of this vision,
The cloud-capped towers, the gorgeous palaces,
The solemn temples, the great globe itself,
Yea, all which it inherit, shall dissolve
And, like this insubstantial pageant faded,
Leave not a rack behind. We are such stuff
As dreams are made on, and our little life
Is rounded with a sleep.
(Prospero, The Tempest, *Act IV, sc. i, 148–158*)

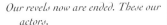

MOURNING RINGS

In his will, Shakespeare left 25 shillings and 8 pence to three of his oldest friends in Stratford and London to buy mourning rings. It was customary to wear mourning rings in memory of a dead friend.

Shakespeare's will

Early in 1616, Shakespeare wrote his will, which still survives today. He left most of his estate to Susanna, including New Place, houses in Stratford and London, and the land he had bought outside Stratford. To Judith, he left a large sum of money and his "broad silver-gilt bowl". He left his sister, Joan, some money, his clothes, and the use of the Henley Street house for life. By right, his wife, Anne, received a third of his estate. Shakespeare also left her "the second best bed", which meant the bed they slept in. The "best bed" was reserved for guests.

Shakespeare's death

Shakespeare is thought to have died on April 23, 1616, on his 52nd birthday. He was buried two days later in Holy Trinity Church, Stratford.

The Gower memorial to Shakespeare in Stratford

Collected Works

Thirty-eight Shakespeare plays have survived to this day. He also wrote poems, including 154 sonnets and three longer works. While it is hard to know the exact date of each work, scholars have come up with approximate dates by consulting documents of the time.

DATES OF SHAKESPEARE'S WORKS

◆ **Plays**
1590–1592 *Henry VI, Part 1; Henry VI, Part 2; Henry VI Part 3*
1592–1593 *The Two Gentlemen of Verona; Richard III*
1592–1594 *The Comedy of Errors*
1593–1594 *Titus Andronicus; The Taming of the Shrew*
1594 *Love's Labour's Lost*
1594–1596 *King John*
1595 *Richard II*
1595–1596 *Romeo and Juliet; A Midsummer Night's Dream*
1596–1597 *The Merchant of Venice; The Merry Wives of Windsor; Henry IV, Part 1*
1598 *Henry IV, Part 2*
1598–1599 *Much Ado About Nothing*

Saving the plays

Shakespeare had his poems published in his lifetime but not his plays. About half of the plays were printed, unofficially, as small paperback books called quartos. Some quartos were based on notes scribbled down during a performance. When the Globe burned in 1613, the actors rescued many precious costumes, props, and Shakespeare's scripts. In 1623 the scripts were collected and published as a book, now called the First Folio. It was the first official collection of plays by Shakespeare. More than 200 copies survive.

A list of actors, including Shakespeare himself, printed in the First Folio

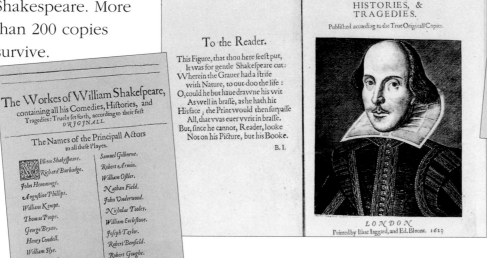

(above) The title page of the Hamlet quarto, 1604

(left) The title page from the First Folio

24

DID YOU KNOW?

In the seventeenth and eighteenth centuries, writers such as Nahum Tate and Colly Cibber rewrote Shakespeare's plays to make them more popular. For example, Tate gave *King Lear* a happy ending, in which Cordelia marries Edgar. (In Shakespeare's original, Cordelia dies.) This version remained the set text for actors for more than 150 years. It was not until the twentieth century that audiences once again saw *King Lear* and other rewritten plays in their original form.

The Sonnets

Sonnets often tell a love story about real people but with false names. Shakespeare's sonnets, first published in 1609, seem to be about the poet's devotion towards a young man and an older woman known as the Dark Lady. The young man may have been Henry Wriothesley, Earl of Southampton, one of Shakespeare's early patrons. Many sonnets are dedicated to "Mr. W. H.," which may be Wriothesley's initials in reverse. Sonnets are short poems of fourteen lines, with a strict system of rhyming. In each group of four lines, alternate lines rhyme (that is, lines 1 and 3, and lines 2 and 4). The last two lines are a rhyming couplet: they rhyme with each other.

The Earl of Southampton, Shakespeare's patron

A new play

In 1998 a historical play written in the early 1590s was generally acknowledged as being a "lost" play by Shakespeare. *Edward III* tells of the early days of the Hundred Years' War between England and France. An American computer analysis of the text and language in seven surviving copies convinced most scholars that the play was Shakespeare's work.

The Histories

Shakespeare's history plays present real characters and events in a dramatic way. This means that Shakespeare sometimes altered facts and dates to suit his plot. These plays focus on themes of war, kingship, and the struggle for power.

The Wars of the Roses

The first group of history plays consists of *Henry VI, Parts 1, 2,* and *3,* and *Richard III.* They cover the period from 1422 to 1485, when the noble houses of Lancaster and York fought for the English throne. The wars are named after their emblems: the white rose of York and the red rose of Lancaster.

O God! methinks it were a happy life,
To be no better than a homely swain.
   (King Henry, Henry VI, Part 3,
         Act II, sc. v, 21–22)

Henry VI, Parts 1, 2, and 3

The three plays about Henry VI look at the problems of weak kingship and the bitter struggle for succession. Henry VI, the Lancastrian King of England and a gentle man, is unable to quash a rebellion masterminded by the Duke of York. To restore peace, he makes York heir to the throne. Civil war follows. York is killed, but his eldest son, Edward, becomes king. Henry is captured and murdered by Edward's brother Richard, who later becomes Richard III.

Henry VI as played by Ralph Fiennes

Richard III

(above) In a film adaptation, Sir Ian McKellen's Richard III rules as a 1930s fascist dictator

(right) Frances Tomalty and Antony Sher in a RSC production of Richard III. Richard is usually portrayed as a hunchback, which was regarded as a symbol of evil in Shakespeare's day

A s Edward IV lies dying, his evil brother Richard plots his own path to the throne. First he disposes of his rivals. His elder brother, the Duke of Clarence, is sent to the Tower of London and killed. Edward's two young sons are also sent to the Tower and later murdered. Richard is crowned king. On the eve of the Battle of Bosworth Field, however, Richard's past returns to haunt him when his victims' ghosts appear. The next day he is killed by Henry Tudor, Earl of Richmond, who becomes King Henry VII.

DID YOU KNOW?

Shakespeare's main source for the history plays was Raphael Holinshed's *Chronicles of England, Scotland, and Ireland*, published in 1577 and revised in 1587. For the early plays he also used *The Union of the Noble and Illustre Families of Lancaster and York* by Edward Hall, which was one of several chronicles commissioned by King Henry VII.

Later history plays

Though written later, the second group of history plays (*Richard II*; *Henry IV, Parts 1* and *2*; and *Henry V*) deals with an earlier period of history. They are set in the years leading up to the Wars of the Roses, from 1377 to 1422. Themes are similar to the first set of plays, but Shakespeare placed more emphasis on the emotions of the leading characters.

Richard II

In Shakespeare's time, being king was seen as a sacred duty, given by God. Such power, however, can lead to a king's downfall. Richard is a weak ruler whose arrogance upsets the nobles he depends on. They side instead with his cousin Henry Bolingbroke. As Richard loses his grip on power, a humbler and more sympathetic man emerges. At the end of the play, Richard surrenders his crown to Bolingbroke.

Jeremy Irons as Richard II

With mine own tears I wash away my balm,
With mine own hands I give away my crown,
With mine own tongue deny my sacred state,
With mine own breath release all duty's rites.
(Richard, Richard II, Act IV, sc. i, 197–200)

Kenneth Branagh plays Henry V in a film version that he also directed

Henry IV, Parts 1 and 2

Bolingbroke becomes King Henry IV, whose son, Hal, spends much of his time drinking with his friend Falstaff. When a rebellion begins, Hal must prove himself worthy of the crown. He kills Hotspur, the rebel leader. At the end of *Part 2*, Hal promises his dying father that he is now reformed. When the king dies, Hal is crowned Henry V.

One RSC production of Henry V *was set during the Second World War*

Henry V

In *Henry V*, Hal declares war on France. At the Battle of Agincourt, the English are heavily outnumbered, but Hal visits the troops and delivers a famous rallying speech. Against the odds, the English are victorious. Hal is portrayed as a model king and soldier. But he is also aware of the human cost of war and of his own responsibilities as king.

The Comedies

Many of Shakespeare's plays are light-hearted, although even the comedies contain tragedy and passion. Often involving mistaken identity, trickery, or love at first sight, the plots of the comedies can be complicated to follow, but they always have happy endings.

The Taming of the Shrew

This is a play about husbands, wives, and marriage. No one will marry bad-tempered Katherine, the "shrew." Although her younger sister, Bianca, has many suitors, custom says Katherine must be married first. Petruchio offers to marry Katherine, whom he calls Kate, then sets about "taming" her. Eventually, she becomes a dutiful Elizabethan wife.

The Merchant of Venice

Needing money to woo Portia, Bassanio asks his friend Antonio for help. Antonio borrows 3,000 ducats from Shylock, a Jewish money lender, agreeing that if he does not repay the loan within three months he must give Shylock a pound of his flesh. A powerful mixture of romance, comedy, and tragedy, the play also looks at the destructive power of racial prejudice.

Fie! fie! unknit that threat'ning unkind brow,
And dart not scornful glances from those eyes
To wound thy lord, thy king, thy governor.
It blots thy beauty, as frosts do bite the meads.
(*Katherine*, The Taming of the Shrew, *Act V, sc. ii, 141–144*)

Shylock (Antony Sher) and his daughter Jessica (Deborah Goodman) in a RSC production of The Merchant of Venice

DID YOU KNOW?

The Comedy of Errors is not only Shakespeare's shortest play (at 1,7/8 lines, it is less than half the length of *Hamlet*), it also includes the most twins – Antipholus of Ephesus and Antipholus of Syracuse and Dromio of Ephesus and Dromio of Syracuse. Throughout the play, one twin is always being mistaken for the other.

A Midsummer Night's Dream

In *A Midsummer Night's Dream*, Oberon, King of the Fairies, uses a magic love potion to end a quarrel with his wife, Titania, and to solve the problems of four young lovers. But the young people, and Titania herself, all end up falling in love with the wrong people. By the end of the play, Oberon and his mischievous servant, Puck, have put things right, and a happy ending is assured.

Titania (Claire Higgins) and Bottom (David Troughton), plus fairies, in a RSC production

Much Ado About Nothing

At first, Beatrice and Benedick are too proud to admit that they are in love. Their time together is spent arguing and outdoing each other with witticisms. Eventually, after being tricked into revealing their true feelings, they resolve their "merry war" and are married. Meanwhile, Claudio and Hero conduct their own, nearly tragic, romance.

Beatrice (Emma Thompson) and others run to meet the homecoming soldiers in a film adaptation of Much Ado About Nothing

As You Like It

The heroine Rosalind falls in love with Orlando, but she is banished from court by her uncle, Duke Frederick. Disguised as a boy called Ganymede, Rosalind and her cousin Celia leave court and enter the Forest of Arden. Orlando is also banished to the forest, where he meets the disguised Rosalind. His brother Oliver falls in love with Celia, and eventually Orlando discovers Ganymede's true identity. The couples are married.

Corin (Colin Douglas), a shepherd, and Rosalind (Juliet Stevenson) in a production of As You Like It

Some are born great, some achieve
greatness, and some have
greatness thrust upon them.
(Malvolio, Twelfth Night, Act II,
sc. v, 132–133)

Viola (Harriet
Walter) is
reunited with
Sebastian (Paul
Spence) in
Twelfth Night

MERRY WIVES

It is thought that
Shakespeare wrote *The
Merry Wives of Windsor*
especially for Queen
Elizabeth I because she
wanted to see the character
of Falstaff (from *Henry IV,
Part 1*) in love. Legend
says that the play took
Shakespeare just fourteen
days to write.

*The merry wives in this
production act their scene
in a hairdresser's salon.*

Twelfth Night

Another romantic comedy of mistaken identity, *Twelfth Night* is set in the imaginary country of Illyria. Viola is shipwrecked and, disguised as a boy called Cesario, she works as a page for Duke Orsino. When Cesario is sent to woo Olivia for his master, Olivia falls in love with Cesario, not Orsino. Meanwhile, Viola's twin brother, Sebastian, arrives in Illyria. Olivia mistakes him for Cesario and marries him. Eventually, all is resolved, and Viola and Orsino are also married.

The Dark Comedies

All's Well That Ends Well, Troilus and Cressida, and *Measure for Measure* are often grouped with the comedies, but the comedy in these plays is much darker. They paint an often disturbing picture of human nature, and the happily-ever-after endings are not all they seem.

*'Twere all one,
That I should love a bright particular star
And think to wed it, he is so above me.*
(Helena, All's Well That Ends Well, *Act I, sc. i, 84–86)*

All's Well That Ends Well

Helena cures the King of France, who, in thanks, offers her Bertram as a husband. He reluctantly marries her then leaves to fight the wars in Italy. He tells Helena he will return only if she can get the ring from his finger and have his child, thinking these tasks impossible. She succeeds through trickery. Reunited with Helena, Bertram remains an unwilling husband.

The French King's court in a traditional production of All's Well That Ends Well *by the RSC*

PLAYING THE FOOL

Fools play an important part in Shakespeare's comedies. They sing, make jokes and puns, and act as messengers for other characters. Feste, the fool in *Twelfth Night*, also turns the tables. His role is to make the audience aware of the foolishness of the main characters. The part was written for Robert Armin, who succeeded William Kempe as chief clown in Shakespeare's company.

Troilus and Cressida

*T*roilus and Cressida* is set during the Trojan War. Troilus, a Trojan prince, loves Cressida, but she betrays him for a Greek soldier, Diomedes. Troilus fails to take revenge. The play ends with the murder of Troilus's brother, Hector. Not a comedy, tragedy, or history, *Troilus and Cressida* is a powerful commentary on the futility of love and war.

Time hath, my lord,
A wallet at his back, wherein he
*   puts*
Alms for oblivion, a great-sized
*   monster*
Of ingratitudes. Those scraps are
*   good deeds past,*
Which are devour'd as fast as they
*   are made,*
Forgot as soon as done.
*   (Ulysses, Troilus and Cressida,*
*   Act III, sc. iii, 139–144)*

The trial scene with Derek Griffiths as Pompey, in a RSC production of Measure for Measure

Measure for Measure

A play about justice and mercy, *Measure for Measure* is set in Vienna, where Angelo sentences Claudio to death for getting Juliet, Claudio's fiancée, pregnant. Claudio's sister, Isabella, pleads for his life. Angelo asks Isabella to sleep with him in exchange for Claudio's life. Isabella refuses. Duke Vincentio intervenes, pardons Claudio, and sentences Angelo to death. Isabella then pleads for mercy for Angelo. Moved, Duke Vincentio spares him.

Haste still pays haste, and leisure
*   answers leisure;*
Like doth quit like, and measure
*   still for measure.*
*   (Duke, Measure for Measure,*
*   Act V, sc. i, 408–409)*

The Tragedies

The tragedies include Shakespeare's most popular and powerful plays. Each one focuses on a tragic hero whose character has a fatal flaw, or weakness, such as jealousy, pride, or indecision. Combined with bad luck, these personal failings inevitably lead to tragic conclusions.

Titus Andronicus

Set in ancient Rome, *Titus Andronicus* is Shakespeare's first and goriest tragedy, a tale of revenge involving Titus, a Roman general, and Tamora, Queen of the Goths. As the play unfolds, Titus's daughter, Lavinia, is raped, and Titus cuts off his own hand in grief. In revenge, Titus kills Tamora's sons and bakes them in a pie, which he serves to their mother.

The pie being presented to Tamora in a production of Titus Andronicus by the RSC

THE TRAGEDIES

Titus Andronicus 1593–1594
Romeo and Juliet 1595–1596
Hamlet 1600
Othello 1604
King Lear 1605
Macbeth 1605
Timon of Athens 1607–1608

---

*It was my dear; and he that
    wounded her
Hath hurt me more than had he
    killed me dead:
For now I stand as one upon a rock,
Environed with a wilderness of sea.*
    (Titus, Titus Andronicus, Act III,
        sc. i, 91–94)

ROMEO AND JULIET

Some famous spin-offs of *Romeo and Juliet:*

◆ In the hit 1957 musical *West Side Story*, composed by Leonard Bernstein, the Montagues and the Capulets become rival gangs, the Jets and the Sharks. The action is set in New York City.

◆ The Royal Ballet's version of the play, choreographed by Kenneth MacMillan and first performed in 1965 in London, starred Margot Fonteyn as Juliet and Rudolf Nureyev as Romeo.

◆ Baz Luhrmann's extremely successful 1996 film starred Claire Danes as Juliet and Hollywood star Leonardo DiCaprio as Romeo.

DID YOU KNOW?

The first woman to play Hamlet was the celebrated French actress Sarah Bernhardt (1844–1923). Nicknamed the Divine Sarah, she was famous for her fiery temper. She played Hamlet when she was fifty-five.

Hamlet is Shakespeare's longest play, with 4,042 lines and 29,551 words. The actor playing Hamlet has 1,569 lines to learn.

The time is out of joint. O cursèd spite,
That ever I was born to set it right!
(Hamlet, Hamlet, *Act I, sc. v,*
189–190)

(below) Kenneth Branagh as Hamlet in a production by the RSC

Romeo and Juliet

Romeo and Juliet marry in secret, but their young love is doomed by the bitter feud between their families, the Montagues and the Capulets. They are also victims of a tragic misunderstanding. Juliet's father wants her to marry Paris. She pretends to agree but takes a sleeping potion that makes her appear dead. Romeo finds her and, believing her dead, kills himself. When Juliet wakes and seeks his body, she stabs herself to death.

Leonardo DiCaprio and Claire Danes played Romeo and Juliet in a 1996 film adaptation

Hamlet

Hamlet's fatal flaw is indecision. He cannot bring himself to kill his uncle, Claudius, who murdered his father. As Hamlet delays, pretending to be insane, he accidentally kills Polonius, whose daughter, Ophelia, goes mad with grief and drowns. Meanwhile, Claudius tries to kill Hamlet but instead poisons the Queen. Hamlet kills Claudius but is fatally wounded in a duel with Ophelia's brother, Laertes, and dies.

A production of Othello *by the RSC*

Othello

*O! beware, my lord, of jealousy.
It is the green-eyed monster which doth mock
The meat it feeds on.*
  (Iago, Othello, *Act III, sc. iii, 169–171)*

In this powerful and moving play, jealousy and issues of race and politics cause a terrible tragedy. Othello, goaded by his friend Iago, becomes convinced that his wife, Desdemona, is having an affair. Eventually his jealousy becomes too much to bear, and he kills her. Too late, he realizes that Iago has lied and, overcome with grief, he stabs himself and dies.

King Lear (Robert Stephens) in a RSC production

King Lear

King Lear decides to divide his kingdom among his three daughters according to how much they love him. Cordelia, the most genuinely loving, refuses to take part in the contest and is banished. Her two sisters, Goneril and Regan, reject their father and quarrel among themselves. When Lear finally sees that what he took for real love is false, it is too late. His family and kingdom have been destroyed.

Is this a dagger which I see before me,
The handle toward my hand?
(Macbeth, Macbeth, *Act II, sc. i, 33–34)*

Macbeth

D riven by ambition and encouraged by his wife, Macbeth murders King Duncan and takes over the Scottish throne. He also kills his friend Banquo. But Banquo's ghost appears to haunt him, and Macbeth is tormented by guilt. Then Lady Macbeth kills herself, unable to live with her conscience. A weak man, Macbeth sinks deeper and deeper into evil. Yet in the end he faces his own death bravely, as the proud soldier he once was.

The real King Macbeth was very unlike the tragic hero of Shakespeare's play. He ruled Scotland wisely and well from 1040 to 1057. Although he did seize the throne from King Duncan, his claim to the crown was as strong as Duncan's. Duncan was also killed in battle, not murdered by Macbeth.

A RSC production of Macbeth. *The figures on the right are the three witches*

DID YOU KNOW?

Many actors believe that any mention of the word *Macbeth* can bring bad luck, so they refer to the work as the Scottish Play. There are stories of *Macbeth* productions in which things have gone wrong. These include the very first performance, when the boy playing Lady Macbeth died.

The Roman Plays

Also known as the Roman tragedies, three plays are set in ancient Rome. They examine the problems of power and politics, the responsibilities faced by leaders of state, and the strengths and weaknesses of historical figures.

Julius Caesar

Fearing Julius Caesar's power, a group of Romans, including Caesar's friend Brutus, rebels against him. On the Ides of March (March 15), they murder Caesar in the Senate. Mark Antony plans to avenge his death. In a stirring speech, he turns the crowd against Brutus. Without support, and guilty about Caesar's death, Brutus cannot live with power. At the battle of Philippi, Brutus and Cassius are defeated and kill themselves.

THE ROMAN PLAYS

Julius Caesar 1599
Antony and Cleopatra 1606–1607
Coriolanus 1607–1608

Friends, Romans, countrymen, lend me your ears.
I come to bury Caesar, not to praise him.
The evil that men do lives after them;
The good is oft interred with their bones.
    (Antony, Julius Caesar, *Act III, sc, ii, 74–77*)

Caesar (Christopher Benjamin) being carried in procession to the Senate in a RSC production of Julius Caesar

---

DID YOU KNOW?

The Roman plays show how Shakespeare sometimes altered the truth for dramatic effect. In *Julius Caesar*, set in the first century, a clock strikes (about 1,000 years before clocks were invented). In *Antony and Cleopatra*, Cleopatra plays billiards (a game that was not invented for another 1,500 years).

Antony and Cleopatra

Antony must choose between his duty to Rome and his love for Cleopatra, Queen of Egypt. To settle a quarrel, Antony marries Caesar's sister, Octavia, but returns to Cleopatra. In the war that follows, Caesar defeats Antony at Actium. Hearing a false report of Cleopatra's death, Antony falls on his sword and dies. Rather than give herself up to Rome, Cleopatra kills herself with a bite from a poisonous snake called an asp.

Elizabeth Taylor and Richard Burton in the classic 1963 film Cleopatra

(below) Coriolanus returns triumphant with his soldiers in a production by the RSC

Coriolanus

The great Roman soldier Coriolanus shows courage and heroism in battle, but these qualities are no preparation for political power. Too proud and snobbish to be a good leader, Coriolanus quickly becomes unpopular. Finally, accused of betraying Rome, he is banished and eventually murdered.

The Late Plays

The plays Shakespeare wrote near the end of his career are romantic comedies. Set in worlds filled with magic and supernatural forces, they focus on characters who are reunited, reconciled, and forgiven for past wrongs.

THE LATE PLAYS

Pericles 1607–1608
Cymbeline 1609–1610
The Winter's Tale 1610–1611
The Tempest 1611

Cymbeline

Cymbeline, King of England, has a daughter, Imogen, whose stepmother wants her to marry her son, Cloten. But Imogen secretly marries Posthumus Leonatus. Thinking Imogen unfaithful, Posthumus orders her killed, but she escapes, disguised as a boy called Fidele. She is reunited with her two long-lost brothers but, thinking Posthumus dead, she joins the Roman invasion of England. The Romans are defeated and Fidele is taken prisoner. But "his" life is spared and all is resolved, and Cymbeline is reunited with Imogen and his sons.

*A father cruel, and a stepdame false,
A foolish suitor to a wedded lady
That hath her husband banished.*
(Imogen, Cymbeline,
Act I, sc. vi, 1–3)

Hermione and Leontes reconcile in a production of The Winter's Tale

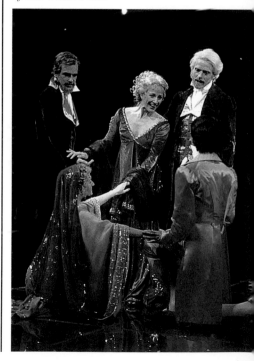

The Winter's Tale

Perdita, as a baby, is abandoned on the shore of Bohemia on the orders of her father, Leontes, King of Sicily, who, in a jealous rage, believed his wife Hermione had been unfaithful to him. When his wife dies, Leontes repents, but it is too late. Perdita is found and brought up by a shepherd. Sixteen years pass. Perdita falls in love with Florizel, son of Polixenes, King of Bohemia, but the king forbids them to marry. The couple flees to Sicily, where Perdita's true identity is uncovered. It is then revealed that Hermione is still alive, and she is reconciled with her husband and daughter.

Miranda and Prospero in a production of The Tempest

O wonder!
How many goodly creatures are
there here!
How beauteous mankind is!
O brave new world,
That has such people in't!
(Miranda, The Tempest, *Act V,*
sc. i, 184–187)

The Tempest

Prospero, the Duke of Milan, and his daughter, Miranda, are cast out to sea by Prospero's wicked brother, Antonio. They are stranded on a distant island, where Prospero uses magic to control the spirit Ariel and the monster Caliban. He also raises a magical storm, or tempest, which brings all his old enemies to the island, including his usurping brother, Antonio; the King of Naples, Alonso; and Alonso's son, Ferdinand. Miranda and Ferdinand fall in love and are married. At the end of the play, Prospero gives up magic, forgives his enemies, and sails for home. Some people think that this represented Shakespeare's farewell to writing.

Performing Shakespeare

Each year hundreds of productions of Shakespeare's plays are staged, from those put on by amateur groups to sell-out tours by the world's greatest theatre companies. Each production is unique; each actor, director, and designer brings individual ideas and skills to the plays.

Choosing a play

The director chooses the play and decides how it should be interpreted and staged. It might be performed in modern dress, in authentic Elizabethan costumes, or in an unusual setting. The director works closely with the actors, guiding them in how to speak their lines and move about onstage.

Preparing for a role

The actors decide how to play their parts to suit the director's interpretation. This means they must know their characters inside out, imagining what makes them think and act as they do. Actors do a great deal of research into the roles and often visit places associated with their plays or their characters.

A PAGE FROM AN ACTOR'S NOTEBOOK
Character notes are based on those made by the actor Philip Voss.

TITLE OF PLAY: *Twelfth Night*

CHARACTER'S NAME: *Malvolio*

SUPER-OBJECTIVE: *To stop being a servant. He wants to rule. He longs for people to be subservient to him.*

OBJECTIVE: *Advancement socially. To lift himself above his station in life.*

LINE OF ACTION: *To do everything he can to please his mistress by complying with ALL the instructions he reads in the letter.*

OBSTACLES AGAINST IT: *The letter is a fake. He is unbelievably gullible and vain.*

PULSE: *Quick*

PHYSICAL CENTER: *The spine*

OTHER VITAL INFORMATION: *One feels his childhood was a struggle—poor and put upon.*

Traditional Elizabethan costumes were worn by Francesca Annis and Barrie Ingham in a RSC production of Measure for Measure

DID YOU KNOW?

Shakespeare's plays include very few stage directions. The most famous direction comes from *The Winter's Tale*, Act III, scene iii. Antigonus lays Perdita on the shore and then leaves, never to be seen again. The stage direction for Antigonus reads, "Exit, pursued by a bear."

Get your apparel together, good strings to your beards, new ribbons to your pumps. Meet presently at the palace ... and, most dear actors, eat no onions, nor garlic, for we are to utter sweet breath.
(Bottom, A Midsummer Night's Dream, *Act IV, sc. ii, 31–40*)

In rehearsal

Rehearsals begin with a read-through of the play. Then the actors work on individual scenes before the whole play is put together. At first the actors read from scripts, but when opening night arrives they must know their lines by heart. They practice in a rehearsal room, not on the stage, and often wear casual clothes while the set and costumes are being designed and made. About a week before the premiere, a technical rehearsal is held to check scene changes and lighting. This is followed by the dress rehearsal in full costume, which is the last chance to make any changes before the curtain rises on opening night.

A young cast rehearses for a RSC production of The Winter's Tale

(left) A modern set design for Romeo and Juliet *at the Royal Shakespeare Theatre in Stratford, England*

(below) Backstage in the RSC wardrobe department

Behind the scenes

P roducing a Shakespeare play is a huge undertaking. Here are a few key members of the backstage team:

STAGE MANAGER: In charge of the actual performances once the play opens; looks after everything on the stage

ASSISTANT STAGE MANAGER: Does a bit of everything: finds props, prompts, and makes sure that the actors are in their correct positions

SET DESIGNER: Designs scenery and stage sets

WARDROBE DEPARTMENT: Designs, makes, and takes care of the costumes

DRESSER: Helps the actors get into their costumes

STAGEHANDS: Put up, take down, and move the scenery

TECHNICIANS: Control lighting and sound

ORIGINAL MUSIC

The only pieces of original music to survive from any of Shakespeare's plays are those for Feste's songs in *Twelfth Night*. These were set on paper by Thomas Morley.

The Royal Shakespeare Company uses about a gallon of stage blood every week. The blood is made from glucose and food dye, sometimes thickened with powder or darkened with treacle (molasses). It must be washable, safe, and pleasant to taste. Breakfast cereal is sometimes added to the stage blood to give extra texture to gory wounds!

Setting the scene

S et design, lighting, costumes, and props all help to create a particular setting and atmosphere. There is no one correct way of setting the background for Shakespeare, and there have been both traditional and modern adaptations of all of Shakespeare's plays. Working from the director's vision, the set designer makes a model of the set. Then the set building begins. The lighting and props must also fit the design.

Dressing the part

C ostumes help set the scene and communicate the personalities of the characters. For example, in the 1993 production of *The Merchant of Venice*, the play was set in a dealing room in the City of London (the financial district), and cast members were dressed as City financiers. To get used to wearing costumes, the actors might wear something similar during rehearsals. At the dress rehearsal, they wear performance costumes.

Some unusual costumes and makeup in a production of The Comedy of Errors *by the RSC*

Shakespeare in Company

Almost 400 years after Shakespeare's death, his plays are still hugely popular all over the world. Many countries have theatres and companies dedicated to Shakespeare's work, and some hold annual Shakespeare festivals.

The Royal Shakespeare Company (RSC)

The world-famous RSC has three theatres in Stratford-upon-Avon, Shakespeare's birthplace. The largest is the Royal Shakespeare Theatre, opened on April 23, 1932 – Shakespeare's birthday. The Barbican Theatre is the RSC's London home. There are two companies, each of about eighty actors, that play in Stratford and London and take plays on national and world tours. They operate on a repertory system, which means that in a single season actors take on several roles in a range of plays.

(above) The Royal Shakespeare Theatre in Stratford at night

The Swan Theatre in Stratford. The RSC also has a third studio theatre, called The Other Place

ON THE NET

If you have access to the Internet, you can find out much more about Shakespeare and his plays. You can try the following sites:
www.rsc.org.uk
www.shakespeare.org.uk
www.shakespeares-globe.org

THE OTHER RSC

The Reduced Shakespeare Company, which began touring in the early 1980s, presents fast, furious, and funny versions of all of Shakespeare's plays in just under two hours. The plays are performed in different styles: for example, *Othello* becomes a rap number.

The Old Globe Theatre in San Diego, California

DID YOU KNOW?

In the former Soviet Union during the Communist age, *Hamlet* was banned because it was feared that the play might cause a backlash against the government. A director who tried to stage the play with music by Shostakovich and a set design by Picasso was arrested and then shot.

Francesca Annis (left) and Judi Dench (right) in a RSC production of The Comedy of Errors

Shakespeare around the world

There are Shakespeare theatres all over the world, including replicas of the Globe in America, Japan, and New Zealand. The Australian and New Zealand Shakespeare Association organizes Shakespeare conferences, lectures, workshops, and master classes. In Canada, a Shakespeare Festival is held each year in Stratford, Ontario. Annual festivals also occur throughout America.

A production of Hamlet *by a Japanese company, directed by Yukio Ninagawa in London*

Famous actors

Many actors have become famous by playing Shakespearean roles. The greatest actor of the eighteenth century was David Garrick (1717–1779). In 1769 he initiated the Shakespeare Jubilee in Stratford, establishing the town as a tourist attraction. In the late nineteenth century, Ellen Terry (1848–1928) starred in the leading female roles. Shakespearean stars of the twentieth century include Laurence Olivier, John Gielgud, Derek Jacobi, Antony Sher, Kenneth Branagh, and Judi Dench.

Famous Speeches

The following are some of Shakespeare's most famous speeches.

HAMLET, ACT III, SC. II, 1–8

HAMLET: Speak the speech, I pray you, as I pronounced it to you – trippingly, on the tongue; but if you mouth it, as many of our players do, I had as lief the town-crier spoke my lines. Nor do not saw the air too much with your hand, thus, but use all gently; for in the very torrent, tempest, and, as I may say, whirlwind of your passion, you must acquire and beget a temperance that may give it smoothness.

AS YOU LIKE IT, ACT II, SC. VII, 139–166

JAQUES: All the world's a stage,
And all the men and women merely
    players.
They have their exits and their entrances,
And one man in his time plays many
    parts,
His acts being seven ages. At first the
    infant,
Mewling and puking in the nurse's arms,
Then the whining schoolboy, with his
    satchel
And shining morning face, creeping like
    a snail
Unwillingly to school. And then the lover,
Sighing like furnace, with a woeful ballad
Made to his mistress' eyebrow. Then a
    soldier,
Full of strange oaths and bearded like the
    pard,
Jealous in honour, sudden and
    quick in quarrel,

Seeking the bubble reputation
Even in the cannon's mouth. And then the
    justice,
In fair round belly with good capon lined,
With eyes severe and beard of formal cut,
Full of wise saws and modern instances;
And so he plays his part. The sixth age
    shifts
Into the lean and slippered pantaloon,
With spectacles on nose and pouch on
    side,
His youthful hose, well saved, a world too
    wide
For his shrunk shank, and his big manly
    voice,
Turning again toward childish treble, pipes
And whistles in his sound. Last scene of
    all,
That ends this strange, eventful history,
Is second childishness, and mere oblivion,
Sans teeth, sans eyes, sans taste, sans
    everything.

ROMEO AND JULIET, ACT II, SC. I, 44–91

ROMEO: But soft. What light through
    yonder window breaks?
It is the east, and Juliet is the sun.
Arise, fair sun, and kill the envious moon,
Who is already sick and pale with grief
That thou, her maid, art far more fair
    than she.
Be not her maid, since she is envious.
Her vestal livery is but sick and green,
And none but fools do wear it; cast it off.
It is my lady; O, it is my love.
O that she knew she were!
She speaks, yet she says nothing.
    What of that?

Her eye discourses; I will answer it.
I am too bold. 'Tis not to me she speaks.
Two of the fairest stars in all the heaven,
Having some business, do entreat her
    eyes
To twinkle in their spheres till they return.
What if her eyes were there, they in her
    head?—
The brightness of her cheek would shame
    those stars
As daylight doth a lamp; her eyes in
    heaven
Would through the airy region stream so
    bright
That birds would sing and think it were
    not night.
See how she leans her cheek upon her
    hand!
O that I were a glove upon that hand
That I might touch that cheek!
JULIET: Ay me!
ROMEO: She speaks, O, speak again, bright
    angel; for thou art
As glorious to this night, being o'er my
    head,
As is a wingèd messenger of heaven
Unto the white-upturnèd wond'ring eyes
Of mortals that fall back to gaze on him
When he bestrides the lazy-puffing clouds
And sails upon the bosom of the air.
JULIET: O Romeo, Romeo, wherefore art
    thou Romeo?
Deny thy father and refuse thy name,
Or, if thou wilt not, be but sworn my
    love
And I'll no longer be a Capulet.
ROMEO: Shall I hear more, or shall I speak
    at this?

JULIET: 'Tis but thy name that is my enemy.
Thou art thyself, though not a Montague.
What's Montague? It is nor hand, nor foot,
Nor arm, nor face, nor any other part
Belonging to a man. O, be some other
    name!
What's in a name? That which we call a
    rose
By any other name would smell as sweet,
So Romeo would, were he not Romeo
    called,
Retain that dear perfection which he
    owes
Without that title. Romeo, doff thy name,
And for that name – which is no part of
    thee –
Take all myself.

HENRY V, ACT III, SC. I, 1–34

KING HARRY: Once more unto the breach,
    dear friends, once more,
Or close the wall up with our English
    dead.
In peace there's nothing so becomes a
    man
As modest stillness and humility,
But when the blast of war blows in our
    ears,
Then imitate the action of the tiger.
Stiffen the sinews, summon up the blood,
Disguise fair nature with hard-favours
    rage.
Then lend the eye a terrible aspect;
Let it pry through the portage of the head
Like the brass cannon; let the brow
    o'erwhelm it
As fearfully as doth a gallèd rock
O'erhang and jutty his confounded base,
Swilled with the wild and wasteful ocean.
Now set the teeth and stretch the nostril
    wide,
Hold hard the breath, and bend up
    every spirit

To his full height. On, on, you noblest
    English,
Whose blood is fet from fathers of war-
    proof,
Fathers that like so many Alexanders
Have in these parts from morn till even
    fought,
And sheathed their swords for lack of
    argument.
Dishonour not your mothers; now attest
That those whom you called fathers did
    beget you.
Be copy now to men of grosser blood,
And teach them how to war. And you,
    good yeomen,
Whose limbs were made in England,
    show us here
The mettle of your pasture; let us swear
That you are worth your breeding –
    which I doubt not,
For there is none of you so mean and
    base
That hath not noble lustre in your eyes.
I see you stand like greyhounds in the
    slips,
Straining upon the start. The game's afoot.
Follow your spirit, and upon this charge
Cry, "God for Harry, England, and Saint
    George!"

RICHARD III, ACT I, SC. I, 1–40

RICHARD GLOUCESTER: Now is the winter
    of our discontent
Made glorious summer by this sun of
    York;
And all the clouds that loured upon our
    house
In the deep bosom of the ocean buried.
Now are our brows bound with victorious
    wreaths,
Our bruisèd arms hung up for monuments,
Our stern alarums changed to
    merry meetings,

Our dreadful marches to delightful
    measures.
Grim-visaged war hath smoothed his
    wrinkled front,
And now, instead of mounting barbèd
    steeds
To fright the souls of fearful adversaries –
He capers, nimbly, in a lady's chamber,
To the lascivious pleasing of a lute.
But I, that am not shaped for sportive
    tricks,
Nor made to court an amorous looking-
    glass,
I, that am rudely stamped and want love's
    majesty
To strut before a wanton ambling nymph,
I, that am curtailed of this fair proportion,
Cheated of feature by dissembling nature,
Deformed, unfinished, sent before my time
Into this breathing world scarce half made
    up –
And that so lamely and unfashionable
That dogs bark at me as I halt by them –
Why, I, in this weak piping time of peace,
Have no delight to pass away the time,
Unless to spy my shadow in the sun
And descant on mine own deformity.
And therefore, since I cannot prove a
    lover,
To entertain these fair well-spoken days,
I am determined to prove a villain
And hate the idle pleasures of these days.
Plots have I laid, inductions dangerous,
By drunken prophecies, libels, and
    dreams,
To set my brother Clarence and the King
Into deadly hate, the one against the other.
And if King Edward be as true and just
As I am subtle, false, and treacherous,
This day should Clarence closely be
    mewed up
About a prophecy which says that "G"
Of Edward's heirs the murderer shall be.

HAMLET, ACT III, SC. I, 58–90

HAMLET: To be, or not to be; that is the
        question:
Whether 'tis nobler in the mind to suffer
The slings and arrows of outrageous
        fortune,
Or to take arms against a sea of troubles,
And, by opposing, end them. To die, to
        sleep
No more, and by a sleep to say we end
The heartache and the thousand natural
        shocks
That flesh is heir to – 'tis a consummation
Devoutly to be wished. To die, to sleep.
To sleep, perchance to dream. Ay, there's
        the rub,
For in that sleep of death what dreams
        may come
When we have shuffled off this mortal coil
Must give us pause. For there's the respect
That makes calamity of so long life,
For who would bear the whips and scorns
        of time,
The oppressor's wrong, the proud man's
        contumely,
The pangs of despisèd love, the law's
        delay,
The insolence of office, the spurns
That patient merit of th'unworthy takes,
When he himself might his quietus make
With a bare bodkin? For who would
        fardels bear
To grunt and sweat under a weary life,
But that the dread of something after
        death,
The undiscovered country from whose
        bourn
No traveller returns, puzzles the will,
And makes us rather bear those ills we
        have
Than fly to others that we know not of?
Thus conscience does make cowards of
        us all,
And thus the native hue of resolution
Is sicklied o'er with the pale cast of
        thought,
And enterprises of great pitch and moment
With this regard their currents turn awry,
And lose the name of action.

SONNET 18

Shall I compare thee to a summer's day?
Thou art more lovely and more temperate.
Rough winds do shake the darling buds of
        May,
And summer's lease hath all too short a
        date.
Sometimes too hot the eye of heaven
        shines,
And often is his gold complexion
        dimmed,
And every fair from fair some time
        declines,
By chance or nature's changing course
        untrimmed;
But thy eternal summer shall not fade
Nor lose possession of that fair thou
        ow'st,
Nor shall death brag thou wander'st in his
        shade
When in eternal lines to time thou grow'st.
So long as men can breathe or eyes
        can see,
So long lives this, and this give life
        to thee.

SONNET 60

Like as the waves make towards the
        pebbled shore,
So do our minutes hasten to their end,
Each changing place with that which goes
        before;
In sequent toil all forwards do contend.
Nativity, once in the main of light,
Crawls to maturity, wherewith being
        crowned
Crookèd eclipses 'gainst his glory fight,
And time that gave doth now his gift
        confound.
Time doth transfix the flourish set on
        youth,
And delves the parallels in beauty's brow;
Feeds on the rarities of nature's truth,
And nothing stands but for his scythe to
        mow.
And yet to times in hope my verse
        shall stand,
Praising thy worth, despite his cruel
        hand.

A MIDSUMMER NIGHT'S DREAM, EPILOGUE

PUCK: If we shadows have offended,
Think but this, and all is mended:
That you have but slumbered here
While these visions did appear;
And this weak and idle theme,
No more yielding but a dream,
Gentles, do not reprehend.
If you pardon, we will mend.
And, as I am an honest Puck,
If we have unearnèd luck
Now to 'scape the serpent's tongue,
We will make amends ere long,
Else the Puck a liar call.
So, good night unto you all.
Give me your hands, if we be friends.
And Robin shall restore amends.

Index

Acknowledgments

Many thanks to Kathy Elgin at the RSC for her help in the production of this book
and for acting as a consultant on the text and pictures. As the result of her help,
many of the images show many of the RSC's most famous faces in action.
Thanks also to Jo Fletcher-Watson in her
unstinting effort in project-editing the book and obtaining the best imagery possible.

The publisher would like to thank all those who supplied photographs for this book.
The copyright owners are listed below:
Donald Cooper c/o Royal Shakespeare Theatre: 37 (left), 38 (right)
Donald Cooper/Photostage: 2, 31
Hulton Getty: 12 (right), 14 (bottom), 16, 20 (left)
Jarrold Publishing: 10 (left), 11, 22, 23, 48 (right)
Joe Cocks Studio Collection/Shakespeare Centre Library: 28
John Tramper c/o Shakespeare's Globe: 6, 18
Jonathan Docker-Drysdale, 1998: 45
Manuel Rivas/Old Globe Theatre, San Diego: 49 (top left)
Kobal Collection: 27 (left), 29 (left)
Renaissance Films/Kobal Collection: 32 (left)
Twentieth Century Fox/Kobal Collection: 37 (right), 41 (right)
Museum of London: 12 (left), 14 (top)
C. Walter Hodges/Museum of London: 13 (left), 13 (right), 17
By courtesy of the National Portrait Gallery, London: 8, 9 (right)
Alastair Muir/Open Air Theatre, Regents Park: 56
Pentagram Design Limited: 15
Press Office, Barbican Centre: 49 (middle)
Press Office, Royal Shakespeare Theatre: 48 (left)
Royal Shakespeare Theatre: 32 (right), 34, 35, 39, 42, 43, 44,
46 (right), 49 (bottom left)
Shakespeare Birthplace Trust Museum: 9 (left)
Shakespeare Birthplace Trust: endpapers, case
Shakespeare Centre Library: 19 (left), 19 (right), 21, 24 (all), 25, 26, 27 (right),
29 (right), 30, 33 (left), 33 (right), 36, 38 (left), 47
Simon McBride 1991 c/o Royal Shakespeare Theatre: 46 (left)
The Trustees of Dulwich Picture Gallery: 20 (right)
Tom Holte Theatre Photographic Collection/Shakespeare Centre Library: 40, 41 (left)

(endpiece) A scene from a RSC production of A Midsummer Night's Dream

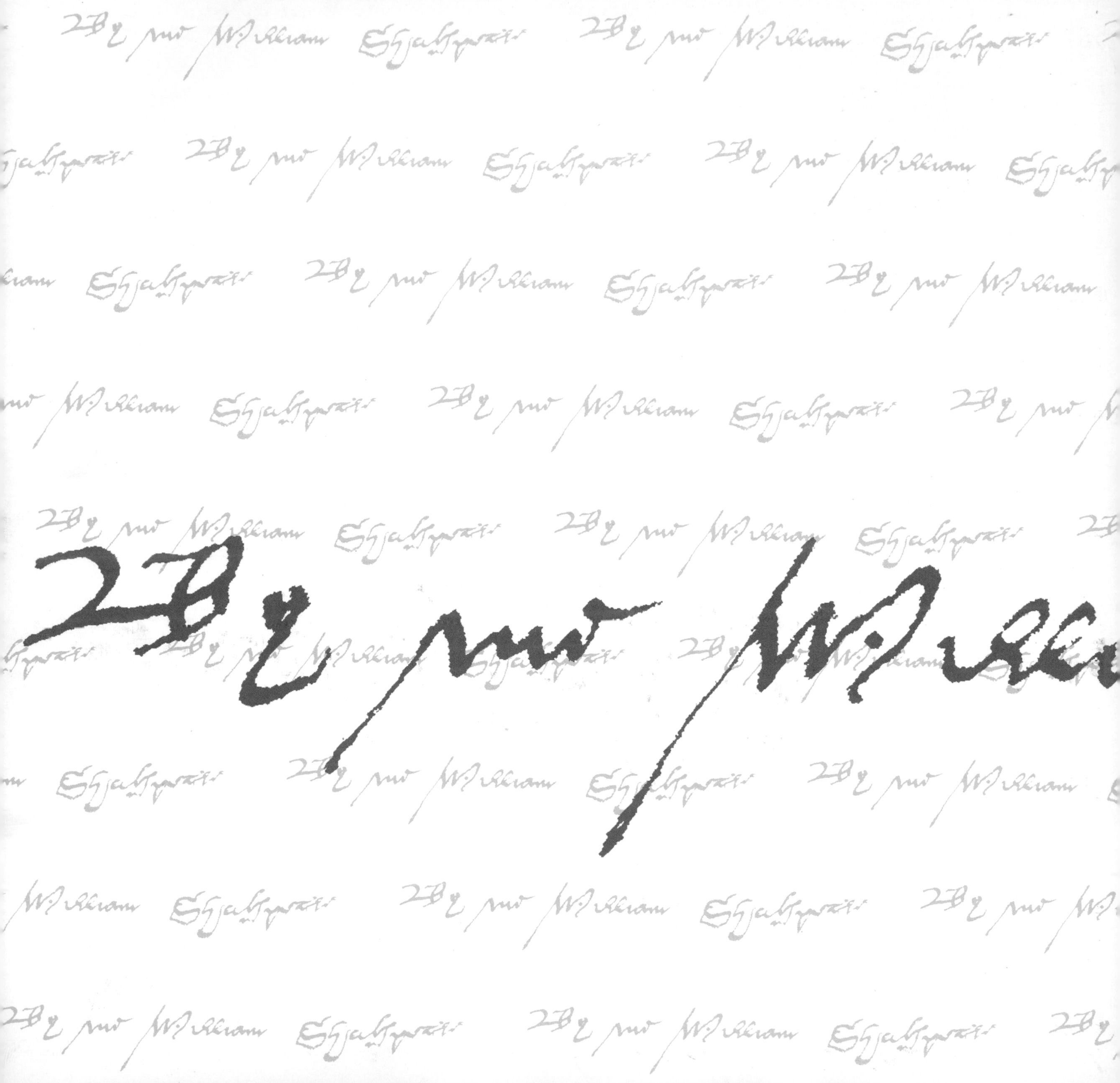